LIVING FAITHFULLY

Living Faithfully: A Journey Through James

Publisher:
Time-Warp Wife Ministries
114 Wyndham Estate Drive
Steinbach, Manitoba
R5G 2K6

Interior design by Darlene Schacht
Cover design by Darlene Schacht

Some images from Adobe Stock Photo

ISBN 978-1-988984-27-8

LIVING FAITHFULLY

A JOURNEY

Through James

DARLENE SCHACHT

TIME-WARP WIFE MINISTRIES

Time-Warp Wife

MINISTRIES

CONTENTS

About the Author:

DARLENE SCHACHT is an award-winning and *NY Times* best-selling author. She is the founder of Time-Warp Wife Ministries, an online publication that encourages women to live Christ-centered lives. Her passion for scripture and hunger for truth is the driving force behind a unique ministry that offers Bible studies and daily marriage prayers.

She began her publishing journey in 2011 working alongside actress/author Candace Cameron Bure to publish *Reshaping it All: Motivation for Spiritual and Physical Fitness.*

With a passion for Jesus, Darlene continues to write, sharing the gospel with countless women around the world.

Visit Darlene's blog at TimeWarpWife.com to find Bible studies, devotionals, and daily marriage prayers.

Other Bible Studies by Darlene Schacht:

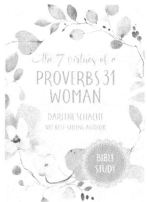

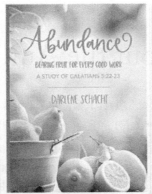

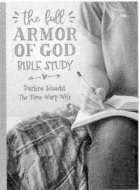

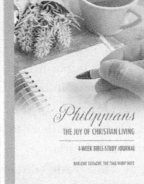

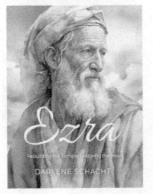

We're delighted to offer supplemental videos for many of our Bible studies. To discover if this study is one of them, please visit YouTube and search for "Time-Warp Wife Bible Studies."

 YouTube

Living Faithfully

Only through faith in Christ does a man learn to do righteously, and to love mercy, and to walk humbly with God; and only by the power of the Holy Spirit sanctifying us to that end do we fulfill these three divine requirements. These we fulfill perfectly in our desire; we would be holy as God is holy, if we could live as our heart aspires to live, we would always do righteously, we would always love mercy; and we would always walk humbly with God. This the Holy Spirit daily aids us to do by working in us to will and to do of God's good pleasure; and the day will come, and we are pining for it, when, being entirely free from this hampering body, we shall serve him day and night in his temple, and shall render to him an absolutely perfect obedience, for 'they are without fault before the throne of God.'

Charles H. Spurgeon

Charles H. Spurgeon, Exposition of Micah 6:8, *delivered on August 22, 1889.*

Introduction

Our first house is what you'd call a starter home. It had charming hardwood floors, French doors that made you feel just a little bit fancy, and a kitchen with black and white checkered flooring that looked like it was straight out of a 50s diner. The bathroom had an old clawfoot tub that added a bit of nostalgia, and there was a faux fireplace that made you feel warm even though it wasn't lit. It had a galley kitchen that sounds far more extravagant than it actually was, and a Dutch door leading out to the back porch—an absolutely adorable little spot to start our life together.

Now, when I tell you that my best friend lived right next door, I mean it literally. Our houses were so close together that I could tap on her bedroom window with my broom when the phone lines were busy—and with dial-up internet back then, they were busy a lot.

For the most part, we loved our little red house on the corner. But, as with many starter homes, there was one big issue—storage. If you had more than one pair of shoes or an extra winter jacket, you had a problem to solve. Our closets were so narrow that you had to angle the hangers just right to fit them in. And a linen closet? Forget about it. We had a dresser that doubled as our TV stand, and one drawer had to hold all of our towels, sheets, and dishcloths.

When our first baby came along, something had to give. There was just no way to fit another bedsheet in that drawer unless I made room. So, I rolled up my sleeves and got to work, taking out the old, tattered rags to make space for the little crib sheets. There wasn't room for both.

Life can be a lot like that little red house—sometimes it gets cluttered with things that just don't belong. We find ourselves holding onto things that we should have let go of a long time ago, and before we know it, there's no room left for what truly matters. That's where the book of James steps

1

in. James is like a wise, practical friend who doesn't just tell us what to get rid of, he shows us what we need to add in its place.

Have you ever wondered what it would be like to sit down with Jesus, to walk with Him, to talk with Him about everyday things? The author of the book of James had that privilege. James, traditionally believed to be the brother of Jesus, grew up in the same house, with the same mother, and shared that unique bond only brothers can have. Can you imagine the impact that must have had on his understanding of faith and life?

But James didn't just keep this wisdom to himself. He became a leader in the early Christian church in Jerusalem, known for his deep piety and practical wisdom. His letter, the Book of James, is filled with down-to-earth advice that speaks directly to our everyday lives. James isn't interested in lofty theological debates; he's concerned with how we live out our faith in real, tangible ways.

James challenges us to put our faith into action, reminding us that faith without works is dead (James 2:14-26). He encourages us to seek wisdom from God, live righteously, and endure trials with patience, knowing that perseverance leads to maturity in our faith. James teaches us about the power of our words, the importance of caring for those in need, and the necessity of living a life that reflects our faith in every area.

The book of James is like that moment when you realize your drawers are too full. It's a call to take out what doesn't belong and make room for what does. It's a challenge to examine our lives and ask, "What needs to go, and what needs to stay?" As we journey through James together, let's be ready to make those changes—to let go of what's cluttering our spiritual lives and embrace the practical, godly wisdom that James offers.

Are you willing to let God transform your life? Are you ready to live faithfully? Me too. Let's get started!

AND WHAT
DOES THE LORD
REQUIRE OF YOU?

TO *Act Justly* AND TO

LOVE
MERCY

AND TO *Walk Humbly*

WITH YOUR GOD.

MICAH 6:8, NIV

Chapter 1

• LIVING FAITHFULLY THROUGH TRIALS •

READ: JAMES 1:1-4 | 1 Kings 18:16-39 & 19:1-18
JOY THROUGH TRIALS

After we grew out of our starter home, we moved less than a block away to a two-story character home. I had been eyeing that house for over a year, wondering if they'd ever sell it and what it would be like to have the extra space for our family. When they finally put it on the market, we carried our boxes down the back lane to our new home on the other corner of the block.

Aside from the extra space, one of the things we loved most about that house was the grapevines that lined the backyard. These grapevines liked to grow, and if left unchecked, they could have easily taken over the yard. As such, my husband Michael was out there every summer pruning and cutting them back, but year after year, they grew even more. Maintaining the vines was a bit of a job, but the abundance of fruit we received was well worth the work.

In much the same way that pruning the vines made them grow and produce even more, the testing of our faith brings about spiritual growth and fruitfulness in our lives. In John 15:2, Jesus said, "He cuts off every branch in me that bears no fruit, while every branch that does bear fruit he prunes so that it will be even more fruitful." (NIV)

What does this process of pruning look like? It could be the removal of distractions or habits that keep us from fully dedicating ourselves to God. It might involve letting go of relationships that pull us away from our faith or stepping back from activities that consume our time but don't contribute to our spiritual growth. Pruning can also mean enduring hardships and trials that God allows to refine our character, teaching us patience, trust, and dependence on Him.

This process isn't easy or pleasant. It might feel like we're losing something valuable or being stretched beyond our comfort zones. But when we allow God to remove the things that hinder our growth, we come out stronger on the other side and better equipped to bear fruit.

James 1:2-4 says, "Consider it pure joy, my brothers and sisters, whenever you face trials of many kinds, because you know that the testing of your faith produces perseverance. Let perseverance finish its work so that you may be mature and complete, not lacking anything."

Notice that James uses the term, "pure joy," or "all joy" depending on what version you are reading. The term suggests that we should find joy in the entire experience of our trials, not just in the parts that are easy to handle.

It's easy to be joyful when life is good, but James is pointing out that it's the hard parts—the struggles and the pruning—that actually build perseverance in us. Just as Michael's careful pruning helped the grapevines grow stronger and more fruitful, our faith is strengthened and refined through the challenges we face. It's like working out a muscle; the more you use it, the stronger it gets. Our faith grows stronger through adversity, and this endurance leads to spiritual maturity.

And here's something I'd like us all to remember: tough times are not wasted times. It's the challenges that help us grow the most. They nurture our faith and build our character. When we persevere through these challenges, we come out the other side more mature and complete. Our faith becomes deeper and more resilient, preparing us to handle future trials with grace and strength.

Charles Spurgeon wrote, "If we were wise, we should begin to welcome trials. We would rather fear to be without them, for up till now, what do we not owe to the furnace, to the rod, to the threshing flail? Scarcely has a mercy of any great spiritual value come to us at all except by the way of the cross... We have been blessed in places of trial, let us not, therefore, dread to go to such places again."

Think about Elijah. He faced immense trials, particularly during his confrontation with the prophets of Baal and while hiding from Jezebel. Imagine the internal struggle he must have felt. Yet, Elijah chose to remain faithful to God, demonstrating incredible perseverance and trust. This test wasn't about God wanting to harm Elijah; it was about proving Elijah's faith and integrity. Just like Elijah, our trials can deepen our faith and trust in God, even when the path is difficult.

Elijah's willingness to go through such challenging trials showed a deep, unwavering faith. This not only strengthened his own faith but also served as a powerful example to others of trusting in God's plan, no matter how difficult it might seem.

Final Thought

Remember, true joy isn't about our external circumstances but about trusting in God's goodness and His plans for our lives. When we truly believe that God is in control and that He wants the best for us, we discover joy on the most difficult days.

? What are some situations in which you felt God was "pruning" you in the past? And, how have these experiences helped you grow in your faith and bear fruit?

. . . .
. . . .
. . . .
. . . .
. . . .
. . . .
. . . .
. . . .
. . . .
. . . .

? James encourages believers to consider trials as 'pure joy' because they produce perseverance. How can this understanding shape your perspective on current or future challenges?

. . . .
. . . .
. . . .
. . . .
. . . .
. . . .
. . . .

KEY CONCEPTS FOR SPIRITUAL GROWTH
JAMES 1:1-4

PERSEVERANCE:

Perseverance refers to the continued effort and determination to do or achieve something despite difficulties, obstacles, or delays. In the context of James 1:4 it is the steadfastness in faith and character that is developed through enduring trials and challenges.

MATURE:

To be mature, in the biblical sense, means to be fully developed in character and faith, reflecting spiritual completeness and growth. It suggests a state of being spiritually strong and equipped, having grown through experiences and trials to a point of wisdom and stability in one's faith.

TESTING:

Testing refers to the process of evaluating or proving the quality, strength, or faithfulness of something. In the context of this passage, the testing of your faith means going through situations or trials that challenge and refine your belief and trust in God. This testing is seen as a way to strengthen and purify faith, leading to greater perseverance and spiritual maturity.

NOTES:

READ: JAMES 1:5-8 | 1 Kings 3 & PROVERBS 3
RELY ON GOD'S WISDOM

My dad was a backyard mechanic, and it was always reassuring to know I had someone to rely on when it came to things I knew nothing about. If my car had a flat tire, he would change it; if I heard a rattle, he would check it; if a taillight went out, he would fix it. I trusted him completely when it came to my car, so if he told me I needed new parts, I'd head straight to the store to get them.

In much the same way, I trust in the Lord. He understands the intricacies of my life far better than I ever could. He has the power to change, check, and fix things in ways beyond my imagination. His wisdom is perfect, and His Word is unfailing. But here's the key to trusting in God: we need to walk in the truth He's given us.

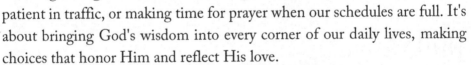

If a mechanic tells me to get an oil change every 5,000 miles, it would be foolish to ignore that advice—especially if I trust him. Wisdom isn't just knowing what's right; it's applying that knowledge in a way that leads to good decisions and actions. What does this look like? It might be choosing to forgive when it's hard, being patient in traffic, or making time for prayer when our schedules are full. It's about bringing God's wisdom into every corner of our daily lives, making choices that honor Him and reflect His love.

James 1:5-8 gives us clear guidance on this. When we lack wisdom, God invites us to ask Him for it—without hesitation or doubt—because He gives generously to all. But we must ask in faith, believing that God will provide the wisdom we need. Faith steadies us, giving us the confidence to face our trials with a sense of purpose and trust in God's plan.

Consider Solomon, who, when faced with the enormous responsibility of ruling Israel, asked God for wisdom rather than riches or long life. God honored Solomon's request, saying, "I will give you a wise and discerning heart, so that there will never have been anyone like you, nor will there ever be" (1 Kings 3:12 NIV). Solomon's wisdom was a divine gift, but it also required faith to apply it rightly.

Prayer is our lifeline. It's the means through which we ask for wisdom, connecting our hearts with God's, seeking His guidance and strength to persevere. When we pray, we express our dependence on Him, trusting that He will guide us through our trials. But James warns us: we cannot afford to doubt. Doubting makes us unstable, like a wave of the sea, blown and tossed by the wind. Our faith must be unwavering, grounded in the certainty that God hears us and will answer.

Trials and challenges reveal the depth of our faith. They expose what's truly going on inside our hearts, sometimes bringing hidden sins or weaknesses to light. And, while God doesn't tempt us with sin, He does allow us to go through tough times that refine and shape us. Even Solomon, despite his great wisdom, made mistakes later in life when he allowed his heart to be led astray. This reminds us of the importance of continually seeking God's wisdom and maintaining a steadfast faith.

Final Thought

The trials we face refine us, and through prayerful reliance on God's wisdom, we gain the strength to endure and grow. Just as Solomon sought wisdom to lead with integrity, we too must seek God's wisdom to navigate our challenges. Trust in His guidance, knowing that His wisdom will lead us to spiritual maturity and a life that reflects His glory.

? Can you identify areas where you might be struggling to fully trust God's wisdom and guidance, and how can you apply James 1:5-8 to grow in faith during these moments?

· ·

· ·

· ·

· ·

· ·

· ·

· ·

· ·

· ·

· ·

? What practical steps can you take to ensure that your decisions are rooted in faith and aligned with God's will, especially when facing trials or challenges?

· ·

· ·

· ·

· ·

· ·

· ·

· ·

· ·

KEY CONCEPTS FOR SPIRITUAL GROWTH
JAMES 1:5-8

WISDOM:

The ability to discern or judge what is true, right, or lasting. In the biblical context, wisdom refers to the knowledge and understanding that comes from God, enabling one to live in a way that is pleasing to Him.

DOUBT:

A feeling of uncertainty or lack of conviction. In the biblical sense, doubt refers to a wavering or lack of trust in God's promises, which can hinder one's faith and relationship with Him.

DOUBLE-MINDED:

Being indecisive or having conflicting thoughts or beliefs. In the Bible, double-mindedness refers to someone who is not fully committed to God, wavering between faith and doubt, leading to instability in their actions and decisions.

NOTES:

READ: JAMES 1:9-11 | MARK 10:17-31
DON'T RELY ON YOUR WEALTH

The other day, we celebrated my grand-daughter's birthday. After a four hour drive, we dropped off our bags at the hotel and each claimed a bed. Call me strange, but after 36 years of marriage, it's nice to have a queen-sized bed all to yourself, not to mention all of the pillows I get to myself! Before heading over to my daughter's place, we had an important stop to make. I wanted to get little Julia her first balloon bouquet, so we went to the dollar store, picked out the prettiest balloons we could find and squeezed them into the back seat of the car.

Julia's face beamed with excitement as soon as we walked through the door, her curiosity quickly following. "How long will they last, Grandma? Will they still be floating when my friends come over this weekend?" I explained to her that while the balloons would stay up for a couple of days, they wouldn't last much longer than that. It was a small but gentle reminder for both of us that earthly treasures don't last, they're here for a moment, then gone, just like those balloons.

This passage from James serves as a powerful reminder of the transient nature of earthly wealth. It's easy to become absorbed in the pursuit of material possessions, but James urges us to remember that these things are only temporary.

He writes, "Believers in humble circumstances ought to take pride in their high position. But the rich should take pride in their humility—since they will pass away like a wildflower. For the sun rises with scorching heat and withers the plant; its blossom falls and its beauty is destroyed. In the same way, the rich will fade away even while they go about their business." (James 1:9-11, NIV)

To illustrate this, let's consider the story of the rich young ruler in Mark 10:17-31. A wealthy young man asked Jesus, "Good teacher, what must I do to inherit eternal life?" Jesus listed the commandments, and the young man confidently replied that he had kept them all. But Jesus, looking at him with love, said, "One thing you lack. Go, sell everything you have and give to the poor, and you will have treasure in heaven. Then come, follow me."

The young man's face fell, and he went away sad because he had great wealth. Jesus used this moment to teach His disciples, "How hard it is for the rich to enter the kingdom of God!" He explained that it's easier for a camel to go through the eye of a needle than for someone who is rich to enter the kingdom of God. Astonished, the disciples asked, "Who then can be saved?" Jesus replied, "With man this is impossible, but not with God; all things are possible with God."

In their cultural context, wealth was often seen as a sign of God's blessing. Even today, some view material prosperity as an indicator of divine favor, which can lead to misplaced priorities. Jesus shifted the focus from human effort to divine grace, teaching us that reliance on wealth will hinder our relationship with God. The story of the rich young ruler highlights the danger of placing too much value on earthly treasures, as his attachment to wealth kept him from following Jesus.

James reminds us that those in humble circumstances should take pride in their high spiritual position. They may not have much in terms of earthly wealth, but their faith and relationship with God are of infinite value. The rich, on the other hand, should take pride in their humility, recognizing that their wealth is temporary and will soon fade away. This isn't to say that wealth is inherently bad, but that our trust and priorities should be rooted in God, not in the fleeting security that wealth provides.

Final Thought:

As we close this section, let's remember that our true worth is not found in material possessions but in our relationship with God. So, whether we find ourselves in humble circumstances or blessed with material wealth, the key is to focus on our relationship with God. He is the source of true, lasting riches. By keeping our eyes on Him, we can navigate the challenges and blessings of life with a heart that treasures what truly matters.

? Why do you think Jesus told the rich man to sell all of his possessions? What was he teaching him by saying that?

? In Mark 10:21, Jesus told the rich young ruler, "One thing you lack." What do you think that "one thing" was?

KEY CONCEPTS FOR SPIRITUAL GROWTH
JAMES 1:9-11

HUMBLE:

Having or showing a modest or low estimate of one's importance. In the biblical context, humble circumstances refer to a state of being lowly or poor, often associated with a dependence on God rather than worldly wealth or status.

PRIDE:

A sense of satisfaction derived from one's own achievements or qualities. In this passage, pride is used in a positive sense, where believers are encouraged to take pride in their spiritual status or position, regardless of their earthly circumstances.

FADE:

To gradually grow faint and disappear. James uses this term metaphorically to describe the transient nature of wealth and the life of those who are rich, emphasizing that worldly success and beauty are temporary and will eventually decline or perish.

NOTES:

READ: JAMES 1:12-18 | 2 SAMUEL 11-12
THE PROGRESSION OF TEMPTATION

Several years ago, before I had children, I was a receptionist at a dental lab. Because I was the first person the customers saw, I liked to dress well. The only problem was that I didn't always wake up early enough to get myself all together. One morning in particular, it was slushy outside. I couldn't find the right boots to wear with a dress, and because the bus was five minutes away, I quickly slipped on a pair of Crocs and ran out the door. It looked silly, but I had a pair of shoes at my desk I could change into once I arrived.

When I stepped on the bus that morning, I noticed two teenage girls look over at my feet, snicker, and whisper something about me to each other. What I should have done was simply let it go, but instead, I spent the rest of the 20-minute ride feeding my anger and nurturing pride. When it was finally time to get off the bus, I walked up to their seat, and like a crazy person, I leaned over and said something critical about the way they were dressed. Thirty-five years later, I still regret letting my anger determine my actions. It was wrong; I knew it then, and I still know it now. That's an ugly and embarrassing story to share, but that's exactly what sin is when it's brought into the light—ugly.

As we read these verses in James, we see that there's a progression with temptation that, when left unchecked, leads us to sin. We all face temptation; even Jesus Himself was tempted by the devil in Matthew Chapter 4. The way we handle temptation determines the result. James tells us, "Then, after desire has conceived, it gives birth to sin; and sin, when it is full-grown, gives birth to death." (James 1:15, NIV)

5 STAGES OF TEMPTATION ACCORDING TO JAMES

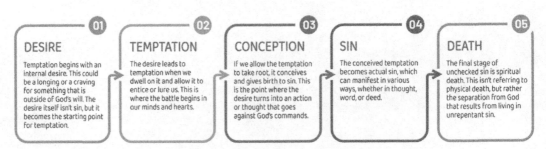

01 DESIRE
Temptation begins with an internal desire. This could be a longing or a craving for something that is outside of God's will. The desire itself isn't sin, but it becomes the starting point for temptation.

02 TEMPTATION
The desire leads to temptation when we dwell on it and allow it to entice or lure us. This is where the battle begins in our minds and hearts.

03 CONCEPTION
If we allow the temptation to take root, it conceives and gives birth to sin. This is the point where the desire turns into an action or thought that goes against God's commands.

04 SIN
The conceived temptation becomes actual sin, which can manifest in various ways, whether in thought, word, or deed.

05 DEATH
The final stage of unchecked sin is spiritual death. This isn't referring to physical death, but rather the separation from God that results from living in unrepentant sin.

When James talks about "conceiving," he's using a metaphor to describe how sin starts in our minds. It all begins with a desire or temptation. This desire is like a seed planted in our thoughts. Whether it's something like greed, lust, anger, envy, or even embarrassment (because you're wearing an ugly pair of Crocs), it starts small, as a thought or an idea.

The word "conceive" here means to form or develop, much like a Polaroid picture that slowly comes into view. When we entertain these desires instead of rejecting them, they start to grow. Think of it like nurturing a weed. If we keep giving it attention and space, it will eventually grow deep roots and flourish. This is what James means when he says desire "gives birth to sin." It's our thought process that nurtures these desires, and if we let them grow unchecked, they lead to actions that go against God's will.

Our thoughts are incredibly powerful. They can rob us of joy, make us anxious, and bring us down. When we dwell on negative or sinful thoughts, they shape our actions. It's like a cycle: sinful thoughts lead to sinful actions, which then reinforce those sinful thoughts, trapping us in a loop. James warns us that when sin is fully grown, it leads to death. This can mean spiritual death, where we feel separated from God, and sometimes even physical consequences that bring destruction into our lives.

Remember David in 2 Samuel chapter 11. He didn't go looking for temptation, but sure enough, temptation found him. Standing on the roof of the palace, he noticed a beautiful woman bathing nearby. Instead of turning away from temptation, he stepped further in. Like so many others who have been in a similar situation, David ignored his conscience and chose to entertain sin. Instead of surrendering himself to God's will by turning away, he defied God by resisting the Spirit and choosing the flesh. When you entertain sin, you fan the flame until you're consumed by its fire.

By sending his servants to inquire about her, David entertained a lust that soon overtook him.

Understanding this helps us realize just how crucial it is to guard our thoughts and desires. By catching and addressing sinful desires early, we can stop them from turning into actions. It's about renewing our minds with God's Word, praying, and asking the Holy Spirit to guide us in transforming our thoughts.

When we persevere through trials and resist temptation, we are not only protecting ourselves from the destructive consequences of sin but also working towards the eternal reward that God has promised us. The crown of life is a symbol of victory and eternal life, given to those who remain steadfast in their love and faithfulness to God. Unlike the fleeting and deceptive nature of temptation, God's gifts are pure, perfect, and everlasting. He is the source of our new life, born through His word of truth, making us a reflection of His creation.

5 Ways to Guard Your Thoughts and Desires:

1. **Renew Your Mind with God's Word:** Spend time daily in Scripture to fill your mind with God's truth.
2. **Pray for Strength:** Ask God to help you resist temptation and guide your thoughts. You should do this daily in addition to the times you're facing temptation.
3. **Stay Accountable:** Share your struggles with a trusted friend or mentor who can support you.
4. **Resist the Devil:** Stand firm against the devil's schemes by refusing to dwell on sinful thoughts.
5. **Focus on the Positive:** Intentionally direct your thoughts to what is true, noble, right, pure, lovely, and admirable (Philippians 4:8).

Final Thought:

Just as David's story teaches us the dangers of unchecked desire, it also reminds us of the importance of repentance and God's readiness to restore those who turn back to Him. Persevere, trust in God's strength, and know that He is with you every step of the way. Through His help, you can overcome temptation and grow in righteousness, ultimately receiving the eternal rewards He has promised.

Reflect on a time when a seemingly small thought or desire led to a sin in your life. Looking back on it now, what could you have done to stop it?

What is "renewing your mind" and how can it help you resist temptation?

. . . .

. . . .

. . . .

. . . .

. . . .

. . . .

. . . .

. . . .

KEY CONCEPTS FOR SPIRITUAL GROWTH
JAMES 1:12-18

PERSEVERES:

To continue steadfastly or determinedly despite facing difficulties or challenges. In this passage, it refers to enduring trials with faith and patience, trusting in God's promises.

TEMPTED:

Being enticed or lured to do something wrong or sinful. The passage emphasizes that temptation does not come from God but arises from one's own evil desires, leading to sin if not resisted.

FIRSTFRUITS:

The earliest or first portion of a harvest, often given as an offering to God. In this context, it symbolizes believers who are brought to new life through God's word, set apart as the first and best of His creation

NOTES:

READ: JAMES 1:19-21, 26 | 1 SAMUEL 25:14-35
QUICK TO LISTEN SLOW TO SPEAK

Several years ago, Michael and I had a friend that we absolutely adored. Even our kids loved the times he spent at our house. There was something about him that made him stand out from the crowd: he had a remarkable way of listening that made you feel like you were the only person in the room. Whenever you spoke, he would lean in, give you his full attention, and respond with genuine interest.

Think about the difference between simply greeting someone at your front door and warmly inviting them into your living room, then you'll get a picture of what he was like. When we truly welcome someone into our home, we offer them a genuine smile, respect, and our full attention. This same principle applies to listening. Listening is more than just hearing words; it's about taking the time to understand and consider what the other person is saying. When you genuinely listen, you embrace their words, value their message, and focus on what they are trying to convey. It's about making the other person feel truly heard and appreciated.

James encourages us to be "quick to listen, slow to speak and slow to become angry, because human anger does not produce the righteousness that God desires." (James 1:19-20) This wisdom highlights the close connection between listening and controlling our anger. Verse 26 adds, "Those who consider themselves religious and yet do not keep a tight rein on their tongues deceive themselves, and their religion is worthless." This reinforces the importance of controlling our speech and the impact it has on our witness and relationships.

Being quick to listen can help you avoid anger and foster peace. While anger can lead to conflict, patience and understanding pave the way for harmony, which will take you much further than anger ever could. By practicing love, holding your tongue, and choosing your words wisely, you create a space for positive interactions. Misunderstandings often lead to anger, so by truly listening, we can avoid jumping to conclusions and becoming upset over things that might not be accurate.

Listening provides a valuable opportunity to connect with others in meaningful ways that you might otherwise miss. It starts with a caring heart. Be thoughtful enough to set aside distractions, considerate enough to lean in and truly hear what the other person is saying, and selfless enough to try to see things from their perspective.

Effective listening is a powerful tool for strengthening all kinds of relationships. It involves creating a space where others feel safe and valued, where their thoughts and feelings are acknowledged and respected. By practicing attentive listening, you demonstrate love and respect, which are essential for any healthy and thriving relationship.

Consider the story from 1 Samuel 25. Nabal, a wealthy but impulsive man, was married to Abigail, a woman of wisdom. When David, who had been protecting Nabal's shepherds, sent his men to request provisions, Nabal's quick temper got the better of him. Insulting David's men and stubbornly refusing their request, provoked an intense reaction from David, who was prepared to attack Nabal's household in retaliation. This rash decision nearly brought disaster upon his entire family, illustrating the dangers of an uncontrolled temper. Proverbs 15:18 tells us, "A hot-tempered person stirs up conflict, but the one who is patient calms a quarrel." Nabal is a perfect example of this, as his impulsive anger led to conflict that could have easily been avoided.

Unlike her husband, Abigail's response was marked by wisdom and patience. When she heard about her husband's reckless behavior, she acted quickly but not out of anger or frustration. Instead, she thoughtfully prepared a generous offering and went to meet David herself. Abigail's calm and measured approach not only averted a potential massacre but also turned David's heart from anger to peace. Her actions highlight the power of a well-timed, thoughtful response, in stark contrast to Nabal's impulsive rage. Their story serves to remind us how important it is to intently listen to others, and to respond with calm and peaceful discernment.

Final Thought:

The next time someone speaks to you, remember to listen with your heart as well as your ears. Show them that their words matter to you, that you value their perspective, and that you are willing to invest the time and effort to truly understand them. This level of listening will deepen your connections and foster more loving, supportive relationships in all areas of your life.

? How can being "quick to listen, slow to speak, and slow to become angry" transform your relationships with others? Can you think of a recent situation where practicing these principles could have led to a more positive outcome?

. . . .

. . . .

. . . .

. . . .

. . . .

. . . .

. . . .

. . . .

. . . .

. . . .

. . . .

? How does effective listening reflect the love and wisdom that God desires in us?

. . . .

. . . .

. . . .

. . . .

. . . .

. . . .

. . . .

. . . .

KEY CONCEPTS FOR SPIRITUAL GROWTH
JAMES 1:19-21 & 26

LISTEN:

To pay attention to or give ear to what someone is saying. In this passage, being quick to listen emphasizes the importance of understanding others before responding, fostering wisdom and patience.

ANGER:

A strong feeling of displeasure or hostility. This passage warns against quickness to anger, as it hinders the righteousness that God desires in our lives.

RELIGION:

A system of beliefs and practices related to worship and devotion to God. Here, it highlights the importance of genuine faith, demonstrated by controlling one's speech and actions, rather than merely outward appearances.

NOTES:

READ: JAMES 1:22-27 | LUKE 10:25-37
ACTING ON FAITH

The other day I was just about to leave the house when I decided to take a last minute look in the mirror. After turning on the bathroom light, I discovered that my blouse was not only on backward, it was also inside out. If you think that's bad, you'll be horrified to know that one day I went outside to mow the lawn with a major wardrobe malfunction. I was out there for a good five minutes before someone in my family told me what I didn't know. It's amazing how something as simple as a glance in the mirror can save us from a lot of embarrassment, isn't it?

This got me thinking about James 1:22-24, where James writes, "Do not merely listen to the word, and so deceive yourselves. Do what it says. Anyone who listens to the word but does not do what it says is like someone who looks at his face in a mirror and, after looking at himself, goes away and immediately forgets what he looks like." Imagine looking in the mirror and realizing that your blouse is on backward. Of course, you're going to fix it, right? If you walked away from the mirror forgetting what you saw, you'd be foolish. That's the point James is making here. Looking at the Bible is like looking in a mirror; it shows us where we need to grow and how we can better serve God.

Consider the story of the Good Samaritan in Luke 10:25-37. Jesus told this parable to illustrate what it means to love our neighbor. In the story, a man is beaten and left for dead by the side of the road. A priest and a Levite, both religious men who knew God's law well, saw the man but chose to walk by without helping. They had the entire Old Testament and the stories of their forefathers to guide them, but they ignored the call to love and assist. They are like the ones who walk away from the mirror, forgetting what they saw.

28

The priest and the Levite might have thought their religious status would save them, but James tells us here what true religion looks like. It's easy to read this story and wonder how they could just walk by, but we need to look at ourselves and ask who we're walking by in our own lives. Who are we ignoring or neglecting, despite knowing God's command to love our neighbor?

The Good Samaritan saw the injured man, took pity on him, and helped him. He bandaged his wounds, took him to an inn, and cared for him. The Samaritan didn't just hear the call to love; he acted on it. This is what James is emphasizing in his letter. Listening alone is not enough; we must also act on what we hear. This means getting rid of moral filth and humbly accepting God's word planted in us.

The Samaritan's actions were a demonstration of true love and kindness. Just as he acted on his compassion and love, we too must act on our faith. His actions weren't just words; they were demonstrated through his care for the injured man. This aligns with what James says about pure and faultless religion: looking after orphans and widows and keeping oneself from being polluted by the world.

Final Thought:

Let's take James' words to heart. Let's not just be hearers of the word, but doers as well. Let's look into the perfect law that gives freedom and continue in it—not forgetting what we have heard, but doing it. In this way, we will be blessed in what we do, and our lives will reflect the love and compassion of Christ.

? What are some areas in your life where you've noticed something that needs to be addressed but haven't yet taken action?

. . . .
. . . .
. . . .
. . . .
. . . .
. . . .
. . . .
. . . .
. . . .
. . . .

? What specific steps can you take to avoid being like the priest and the Levite, who knew the truth but failed to act on it?

. . . .
. . . .
. . . .
. . . .
. . . .
. . . .
. . . .
. . . .
. . . .
. . . .

KEY CONCEPTS FOR SPIRITUAL GROWTH
JAMES 1:22-27

PERFECT LAW:

The complete and flawless set of instructions or principles given by God, particularly as revealed in the New Testament. In this passage, the "perfect law" refers to God's commands, which are designed to guide believers toward righteousness and spiritual freedom. It suggests that living according to this law leads to true liberty and blessings in one's life.

FREEDOM:

The state of being free from bondage, oppression, or restraint. The passage refers to the "perfect law that gives freedom," which implies that true freedom is found in living according to God's word, leading to a life that aligns with His will.

POLLUTED:

Contaminated or tainted by harmful substances or influences. In this passage, it is used metaphorically to describe the moral or spiritual defilement that can occur when one is influenced by the sinful practices and values of the world.

NOTES:

Chapter 2

· LIVING FAITHFULLY THROUGH ACTIONS ·

READ: JAMES 2:1-13 I LUKE 16:19-31
INCLUSIVE AND IMPARTIAL LOVE

When I was expecting our second child, I was somewhat concerned. I know you'll probably think I'm being silly for even saying this out loud, but the truth is, I didn't think I could love another child as much as I loved my first born. Brendan had been with us for six years before Madison came along. He was my baby boy, my snuggle bug, my thumb-wrestling buddy. How could anyone possibly fill his shoes when my heart was already bursting with love?

And then it happened. On one chilly December morning, I fell in love all over again. The moment they put her in my arms, my heart expanded in a way I never thought possible. Madison's tiny fingers wrapped around mine, and I realized that love isn't about dividing—it's about multiplying. Both children were unique, and my heart had plenty of room for both.

A year later, Graham was born (we like to call him G), and two years after that, our sweet and goofy Nathaniel. The ability to open my heart, and open it much wider yet, has shown me the boundless and ever-expanding power of love. A love that always protects, always hopes, and always endures. Could I ever pick one that I favor the most? Not a chance. They don't compete for space in my heart; they complement and enrich it in their own unique way.

The things we see and touch have limits. There's only so much room in the house, so much money in the bank, and so much food in the fridge, so we ration, budget, and save. When someone moves in, you divide your existing space to make room. But the heart is different, my friend. Instead of dividing our love, our capacity to love expands.

When we realize that our love, like God's, has the capacity to expand beyond our understanding, we can begin to embody the principles of mercy and equality that James emphasizes. By embracing this boundless love, not just within the walls of our home but in every aspect of our lives, we reflect God's inclusive and impartial love, treating everyone with the same kindness and respect we'd want others to show us.

The dangers of showing favoritism are powerfully illustrated in the story of the rich man and Lazarus from Luke 16:19-31. The Bible tells us that the rich man lived in luxury while Lazarus, a poor man, lay at his gate, longing for the scraps from the rich man's table. Despite their proximity, the rich man showed no compassion or mercy towards Lazarus. When both men died, Lazarus was carried by angels to Abraham's side, while the rich man found himself in torment in Hades. The rich man's favoritism and lack of compassion led to his ultimate suffering, highlighting the importance of treating everyone with equal love and respect.

This story echoes the message in James 2:1-13, reminding us to be inclusive and impartial, and to love our neighbors as ourselves. Chances are, you're not a rich woman living in luxury while a poor man lies at your gate, but perhaps you find yourself favoring certain friends over others, prioritizing those who are similar to you or who are easier to spend time with. Maybe at church, you give more attention and opportunities to those who are more outgoing or who share your interests, unintentionally neglecting others who are quieter or different.

It's natural to have close friends and people you connect with more easily. However, it's also important to make an effort to include others and to reach out to those who might feel left out. Take the time to get to know people who are different from you, and be intentional about showing kindness and making space for them in your life. Small acts of inclusion and kindness can make a significant impact in someone's life, and in many cases, draw them closer to Christ.

Final Thought:

By expanding our hearts and embracing a love that goes beyond our understanding, we can avoid the pitfalls of favoritism and truly embody the principles of mercy and equality that God calls us to live by. This boundless love not only enriches our lives but also reflects God's grace and inclusivity, bringing us closer to His ideal of treating every person with dignity and respect.

What are some modern-day examples of favoritism in our communities or churches? How can we guard against this in our own lives?

In what ways have you noticed yourself showing favoritism, either in your family, friendships, or church community? How can you work towards being more inclusive?

KEY CONCEPTS FOR SPIRITUAL GROWTH
JAMES 2:1-13

FAVORITISM:

The practice of giving unfair preferential treatment to one person or group at the expense of another. In this passage, favoritism refers to showing partiality based on external factors such as wealth or status, which is condemned as incompatible with the teachings of Jesus.

KINGDOM:

Refers to the reign or rule of God, especially in a spiritual sense, where those who love Him and follow His teachings will inherit eternal life. The "kingdom" here denotes the spiritual inheritance and blessings promised by God to those who are faithful, regardless of their worldly status.

LAW:

The commandments or rules given by God, particularly those found in the Old Testament, that dictate moral and religious conduct. In verse 10, "law" refers to the entirety of God's moral law, indicating that breaking even one part of it makes one guilty of breaking the whole law. This differs from the "perfect law" mentioned earlier, which focuses on the New Testament teachings and the law of liberty that leads to spiritual freedom.

NOTES:

READ: JAMES 2:14-26 | GENESIS 22 & JOSHUA 2
FAITH WITHOUT WORKS

Every morning before leaving for work, Michael used to walk over to my side of the bed, tuck me in, kiss my forehead, and tell me he loved me. He's retired now, but I still get kisses throughout the day along with gentle reminders that whisper "I love you." The beautiful thing about those three little words is that they're backed up with actions day after day.

Michael likes to do things to show me he's been there and how much he cares. Some days he's sweet, and other days he's just silly, like the time he put his toolbox under my pillow (I didn't notice until about 2am). Or the day he tied all of my hairbrushes together with elastic bands. He hides my toothpaste, moves my toothbrush, and builds a five foot tower of toilet paper when all that I needed was one. He puts Q-Tips in my makeup bag, chocolate bars on my desk, and candy in the cupboard. Just last night he put every pillow he could find on my side of the bed.

He goes the extra mile to give me warm hugs and hot chocolate on cold winter nights. He buys me spring flowers, sits on the deck with me on warm summer nights, and cleans up our yard in the fall. His thumbprints are everywhere, speaking louder than words.

Words are meaningless if we don't back them up, aren't they? If we say that we care, but every action we take clearly shows that we don't, we're just full of hot air. In the same way that words without action are empty, faith without works is dead.

So, what is faith exactly? Does it mean that you believe in God? Yes, but there's more to it than that. The words faith and belief are often used synonymously, but they have important distinctions. Belief is simply accepting that something is true. For example, you might believe that God exists. Faith, however, goes beyond belief. Faith involves trust, reliance, and acting on that belief. True faith manifests in actions that demonstrate our trust in God.

Notice what James says in 2:19: "You believe that there is one God. Good! Even the demons believe that—and shudder." James is pointing out the fact that belief alone is insufficient, as even demons acknowledge the existence of God. What sets faith apart is the elements of trust and obedience, leading to a life that reflects God's teachings and commands. Genuine faith compels us to live out our convictions through tangible actions that glorify God and serve others.

What does that look like in our everyday lives? James gives us an example in this chapter when he writes, "Suppose a brother or a sister is without clothes and daily food. If one of you says to them, 'Go in peace; keep warm and well fed,' but does nothing about their physical needs, what good is it? In the same way, faith by itself, if it is not accompanied by action, is dead" (James 2:15-17, NIV).

Faith is the conviction of truth, and when we're truly convicted that Jesus is Lord, faith is at work in our lives—moving, serving, and pleasing Him with all that we do, even when our faith calls us to the altar of sacrifice.

James gives us two examples of genuine faith in this chapter: Abraham and Rahab. In Genesis 22, God tests Abraham by asking him to sacrifice his beloved son Isaac. Despite the heart-wrenching nature of this command, Abraham obeyed God, demonstrating his faith through his actions. As he prepared to sacrifice Isaac, an angel of the Lord stopped him and provided a ram as a substitutionary sacrifice. Abraham's willingness to go to such lengths showed his profound trust and obedience to God.

Similarly, Rahab took an enormous risk by hiding the Israelite spies and helping them escape. Her actions in Joshua chapter 2 were a demonstration of her faith and trust in the God of Israel. Because of her faith, Rahab and her family were spared during the fall of Jericho, and she became part of the lineage of Jesus.

A more recent example that comes to mind is our dear sister in Christ, the beloved Corrie ten Boom. During World War II, Corrie and her family risked their lives to hide Jews from the Nazis, driven by their unwavering

Christian faith and deep belief in the dignity and worth of every human being. Even after being arrested and sent to a concentration camp, Corrie's faith didn't falter. She continued to share the love of Christ with her fellow prisoners, offering hope and comfort in one of the darkest places imaginable. Her steadfast faith and commitment to living out the teachings of Jesus spoke louder than words ever could.

Every day we see opportunities to shine in this world and to live out our faith. It could be something as simple as giving up a Saturday to help a friend move, offering a listening ear to someone in distress, volunteering at a local shelter, or sharing a meal with someone in need. These small sacrifices are powerful demonstrations of our faith in action, showing the love of Christ through our deeds.

The lyrics from Casting Crowns' song "If We Are the Body" challenge us to reflect on our actions and ask ourselves if we're living by the faith we profess:

"If we are the body,
Why aren't His arms reaching?
Why aren't His hands healing?
Why aren't His words teaching?"

Looking at people like Abraham, Rahab, and Corrie ten Boom, we see how actions reveal the depth of one's faith. Three living testimonies of strength that inspire us to step out boldly and live out our faith with unwavering conviction and grace. Their examples encourage us to trust God fully, live out the faith we profess, and spread the gospel of Christ.

Final Thought:

Let's not be content with merely believing. Let's be doers of the Word, allowing our faith to move us to action. By serving others with the gifts and resources God has entrusted to us, we become living testimonies of His grace and love. It's through these acts of faith that we can make a real, lasting impact on the lives of others around us.

What is the difference between belief and faith? How does understanding this difference influence the way we live out our faith in practical ways?

Can you share a time when someone's actions spoke louder than their words in your life?

KEY CONCEPTS FOR SPIRITUAL GROWTH
JAMES 2:14-26

FAITH:

Complete trust in God and His promises. In this passage, faith manifests in actions that demonstrate our trust in God. True faith goes beyond intellectual agreement and is demonstrated by living according to God's love and commands. Faith without deeds is considered "dead," meaning it is not active or living.

BELIEVE:

To accept something as true, particularly the belief in God's existence and His attributes. In this passage, belief is acknowledged as essential, but the writer of James points out that even demons believe in God—yet this belief alone does not lead to salvation. Belief must be coupled with faith that transforms one's actions and life.

DEEDS:

Actions that reflect one's faith in God, often called "works" or "good deeds." Deeds are the visible evidence of true faith, showing that belief is genuine. While they do not earn salvation, they naturally flow from faith and are essential in demonstrating a believer's relationship with God.

NOTES: . . . .

. . . .

. . . .

. . . .

. . . .

Chapter 3

· LIVING FAITHFULLY THROUGH WORDS ·

READ: JAMES 3:1-12 | 2 KINGS 5:1-15
THE DANGERS OF AN UNBRIDLED TONGUE

As someone who loves to talk, I've come to learn that words can be both a blessing and a burden at times. Graham, the quietest one of our four kids, used to say, "Why waste words when you don't have to?" Unlike my son, I see words like a box of crayons—why settle for 8 when you have 96 beautiful colors to choose from? I'd use them all if I could, but when I open my Bible, I find a different approach: "My dear brothers and sisters, take note of this: Everyone should be quick to listen, slow to speak and slow to become angry" (James 1:19, NIV).

Listening gives us the opportunity to connect with others on a deeper level. It's about ensuring they feel respected and cherished. It's not just about hearing; it's about considering the words of another and also considering ours. We might not always agree, but patience and understanding will take us further than anger and spite ever could. Have you ever felt that urge to snap back with a quick retort when someone says something hurtful? I've definitely been there. But over time, I've learned the wisdom in pausing because I've seen firsthand the damage that a hasty word can cause. We all know that an unconstrained tongue resolves nothing; it's the gentle and quiet spirit that mends fences, softens hearts, and ministers grace. Pay close attention to this verse, because it's so relevant to the times we live in today. With so much division and everyone ready to jump on their soapbox, we need to take this to heart: Proverbs 10:19 reminds us, "Sin is not ended by multiplying words, but the prudent hold their tongues" (NIV). Before speaking or typing, let's ask ourselves: Does this glorify God? Does it point others to Christ? Does my response align with the fruit of the Spirit? If it doesn't, maybe it's better left unsaid.

We read the Bible, and for most of us, we know what we should and shouldn't be saying. We might even give silence a sincere shot, but then, out of nowhere, our tongue takes control, and we end up saying things we instantly regret. As I got to thinking about that today, I was reminded of the story from 2 Kings chapter 5. Naaman, a valiant soldier and commander of King Aram's army, had leprosy. After a young Israelite girl told Naaman that he could be healed, he sought healing from the prophet Elisha.

Further into the story, we see that when things didn't go the way that Naaman expected, he lost his temper instead of humbling himself before God. The Bible tells us, "Elisha sent a messenger to say to him, 'Go, wash yourself seven times in the Jordan, and your flesh will be restored and you will be cleansed.' But Naaman went away angry and said, 'I thought that he would surely come out to me and stand and call on the name of the Lord his God, wave his hand over the spot and cure me of my leprosy. Are not Abana and Pharpar, the rivers of Damascus, better than all the waters of Israel? Couldn't I wash in them and be cleansed?' So he turned and went off in a rage" (2 Kings 5:10-12, NIV).

After listening to the wise counsel of his servants, Naaman made a choice to humble himself and turn back. Then, after dipping himself in the Jordan River seven times as the man of God had instructed, Naaman was healed. It's sad how pride and anger can take such a toll on our lives. Once those emotions form words and roll off of our tongues they can divide friendships, destroy families, hinder our testimonies as a believers, and in Naaman's case, it almost cost him his healing. Matthew 15:18 reminds us, "But the things that come out of a person's mouth come from the heart, and these defile them" (NIV). This verse reminds us that taming the tongue begins within our hearts and works its way out. We need to put down our pride and control our anger before it rolls off of our tongue.

If we're kind on the outside but rotten on the inside, we're just like the Pharisees who followed the letter of the law yet neglected the more important things of God like mercy, kindness, and love. They were meticulous about cleaning the outside of their cups, but inside, they were full of greed and self-indulgence. Paul advises us, "Get rid of all bitterness, rage and anger, brawling and slander, along with every form of malice. Be kind and compassionate to one another, forgiving each other, just as in Christ God forgave you" (Ephesians 4:31-32, NIV). If only we truly embraced this verse, we would see a transformation not just in our own lives, but also in the lives of those around us. Kind and compassionate words stem from a heart that has been purified by the love and grace of Christ. When we release bitterness and anger, we create space for the Holy Spirit to work within us and through us, affecting the way that we speak, and the way we treat others. As we close this chapter I'd like to leave you with this final word of encouragement:

> *Be wise in the way you act toward outsiders; make the most of every opportunity. Let your conversation be always full of grace, seasoned with salt, so that you may know how to answer everyone. - Colossians 4:5-6*

Final Thought:

Our words hold tremendous power. They can build up or tear down, heal or hurt, inspire or incite. James's admonition to control our tongues is not just about avoiding hurtful speech, but about cultivating a heart that seeks to honor God and uplift others. As we navigate our daily interactions, let's strive to speak words that reflect Christ's love and grace. In doing so, we can be a light in a world often darkened by harsh and hasty words.

Colossians 4:5-6 encourages us to have conversations "full of grace, seasoned with salt." What does this look like in practice, especially when interacting with those who don't share our faith?

Can you recall a situation where holding your tongue led to a better outcome? How did this decision affect your situation?

. . . .

. . . .

. . . .

. . . .

. . . .

. . . .

. . . .

. . . .

KEY CONCEPTS FOR SPIRITUAL GROWTH
JAMES 3:1-12

PERFECT:

In this context, "perfect" refers to spiritual and moral completeness or maturity. It doesn't imply flawlessness in the absolute sense but rather the ability to exercise complete self-control, especially over one's speech. A "perfect" person in this passage is someone who can control their tongue, which is seen as a sign of overall maturity and discipline.

STUMBLE:

To stumble means to make a mistake or fall into sin. In the passage, it refers to the various ways in which people can fail, particularly in their speech. The idea is that everyone stumbles or errs in many ways, but those who can control their words are less likely to stumble and are on the path toward spiritual maturity.

JUDGED:

To be judged is to be evaluated or assessed, often in a moral or spiritual sense. In this context, those who teach are cautioned that they will be judged more strictly, meaning they are held to a higher standard because of the influence and responsibility they carry in guiding others.

NOTES:

. . . .

. . . .

. . . .

. . . .

. . . .

. . . .

READ: JAMES 3:13-18 | JOHN 13:1-30
EXAMINE YOUR HEART

I received a sweet gift from a friend one day. The girl who lives with us walked over to me with a green plastic bag, and said, "I'm cleaning your car, and I don't want you to say 'no.' I know you've been stressed out lately, and so I want to do this for you."

First off, let me tell you that my car was a mess. One look in the window and you would have quickly agreed. There were French fries on the floor in the back, flyers scattered throughout, and a few lost mittens thrown here and there. The dashboard hadn't been wiped down in who knows how long, and to top it all off, it was loaded with dog hair.

In my defense, my son borrows my car a lot, winters are freezing up here, and this winter was exceptionally cold. Standing in snow, cleaning the car has been the last thing on my mind. Besides that, I'm a bit of a car slob sometimes.

As embarrassing as it is, some days you just have to accept a gift and say, "thank you." So, I did, but not without a gift in exchange.

"Okay, but what can I do for you?" I asked. "Can I clean your room?"

She agreed. And so, for the next hour or so, we rolled up our sleeves and got to work blessing each other.

In chapter 2, James emphasized the relationship between faith and deeds, illustrating that actions go hand in hand with our faith. He takes it a step further in this chapter by examining the attitude of our hearts, pointing out that selfish ambition and envy are both earthly and unspiritual. The attitude of our heart is just as important as the actions themselves, if not more so. Both our words and our deeds should align with the "wisdom that comes from above," which James describes this way: "But the wisdom that comes from heaven is first of all pure; then peace-loving, considerate, submissive, full of mercy and good fruit, impartial and sincere" (James 3:17, NIV).

Proverbs 16:2 tells us, "All a person's ways seem pure to them, but motives are weighed by the LORD."

People do good work for all kinds of reasons. They volunteer at church, give to the poor, and help those in need. The question we need to ask ourselves is, what is the motive behind my actions? Are they driven by selfish ambition and pride, a desire for recognition, or the love of money? Or are they motivated by a genuine love for God?

I'm embarrassed to say that there have been times when selfish ambition was driving my cart. We love God, but at the same time, many of us crave the validation that comes from being recognized. The real test of our faith comes in those quiet moments when no one but God sees the sacrifices we make. James isn't discouraging us from doing good deeds; rather, he's urging us to examine what's in our hearts: are we willing to give when nobody knows? If so, will we give just as much? Are we willing to help without recognition? When we do good solely because we love God, we reflect His love and grace.

Philippians 2 tells us to put on the mind of Christ, who took on the form of a servant and humbled Himself before God and man. In the same chapter, Paul writes, "Do nothing out of selfish ambition or vain conceit, but in humility consider others better than yourselves. Each of you should look not only to your own interests, but also to the interests of others." (Philippians 2:3-4, NIV)

I can clean my home, cook a meal, and take care of my family, but if I'm not doing it for the right reasons, then I'm merely doing a job. Sure, we can do our job and also be a servant at the same time, but we can also do a job and not be a servant at all.

We've read how our Savior washed the disciples' feet on the night He was betrayed. We read how He went to the cross like a lamb to the slaughter, and how He gave up His life for ours. The key there is the disregard of one's own interest. What's most incredible about the events in John chapter 13 is the order in which they took place. Notice that Jesus washed their feet after the devil prompted Judas to betray Him. Jesus knew this full well when He got up from His meal. In fact, He mentioned it to the disciples right after He was done. He didn't wash 11 men and skip the 12th. He put Himself aside to serve them all. Why? Because He loved His Father with all of His heart, soul, strength, and mind, and loved His neighbor as Himself.

It's in those unseen acts of kindness, those moments of sacrifice, when we serve without any expectation of recognition or reward, that our faith shines brightest. True wisdom and humility are displayed when we act out of pure love for God, allowing our deeds to be a testament to His presence in our lives. Let's strive to purify our hearts, setting aside selfish ambition and pride, so that we can serve others with genuine love and humility. When we do, we are truly walking in obedience to His greatest commandment: to love the Lord our God with all our heart, soul, strength, and mind, and to love our neighbors as ourselves.

Final Thought:

Our actions should stem from a genuine love for God and a desire to serve others selflessly. By examining our motives and setting aside selfish ambition and pride, we can allow God's love and grace to shine through us. Let our deeds be a testament to His presence in our lives, demonstrating our faith through humble and sincere service.

How does Jesus' example of washing the disciples' feet, including those who would betray or deny Him, challenge our approach to serving others?

Think about a recent act of service or kindness you performed. What was your motive behind it, and how can you continue to grow in aligning your actions with the humility and selflessness exemplified by Jesus?

KEY CONCEPTS FOR SPIRITUAL GROWTH
JAMES 3:13-18

EARTHLY WISDOM:

Earthly wisdom is rooted in worldly values, characterized by selfishness, pride, and a focus on personal gain. It is described as unspiritual and demonic, leading to disorder and evil practices. This wisdom is disconnected from God's truth and is concerned with temporary, material concerns rather than eternal, spiritual ones.

HEAVENLY WISDOM:

Heavenly wisdom is wisdom that comes from God and reflects His character and values. It is pure, peace-loving, considerate, submissive, full of mercy and good fruit, impartial, and sincere. This wisdom leads to righteousness, peace, and a life that honors God. It is marked by humility and the desire to do good for others.

SELFISH AMBITION:

Selfish ambition refers to the pursuit of personal gain or success at the expense of others, often driven by a desire for power, recognition, or advantage. In the passage, selfish ambition is associated with envy and is contrasted with the humility that comes from true wisdom. It is seen as a destructive force that leads to disorder and evil practices.

NOTES:

Chapter 4

• LIVING FAITHFULLY THROUGH HUMILITY •

READ: JAMES 4:1-3 | MATTHEW 3 & JOHN 3:22-30
MORE OF HIM, LESS OF US

Growing up in the 70s, there was a tradition among many families, and a day that every child looked forward to. The arrival of the Sears Christmas catalog. The catalog, also known as the "Wish Book," was glossy, colorful, full of possibilities, and unlike today's slim flyers, this catalog was hefty! The day it  arrived, my sisters and I would grab our pens and take turns flipping through the pages, circling all of the toys we wanted Santa to bring us. Even though our parents rarely bought us what we circled, the joy of dreaming kept us coming back year after year.

While this might seem a bit selfish in hindsight, many of us approach prayer the same way. We present our desires to the Lord, almost like a wish list, hoping He'll fulfill them. James opens this chapter by talking about the desires that battle within us. Whether we're praying or interacting with others, there's this deep-seated desire to get what we want. Why do we fight, gossip, or put others down? Because, let's be real, we think there's something in it for us. It might be protecting our pride or elevating ourselves to gain the admiration of others. James is pointing out that these desires for pleasure often drive our actions, even our prayer life.

Depending on your Bible translation, you might see the word "desire" or "lust" used a few times in this chapter. The Greek word "hēdonē" translates to "pleasure" or "desire for pleasure." Throughout scripture, this word often carries a negative tone, pointing to pleasures that can lead us into sin.

James highlights two common issues among believers:

1. **Lack of Commitment to Prayer:**
    "You do not have because you do not ask God."
    This suggests that we miss out on certain things simply because we're not asking God for His help or provision.

2. **Impure Motives in Prayer:**
    "When you ask, you do not receive, because you ask with wrong motives."
    We might be asking for things driven by selfish desires instead of aligning with God's will.

Recognizing these unhealthy desires is the first step to overcoming them. The next step? Doing something about it. One practical way to start is by reflecting on our motives before we pray. Are we seeking His will or just pursuing our own interests? Are we more focused on what we want, or are we asking God what He wants? Honestly, if I got everything I've ever prayed for, I'd have missed out on the blessings around me now, not to mention I'd be miserable. I've had some pretty bad ideas over the years, and I'm grateful that God led me in a different direction. When we pray, we must be willing to submit ourselves to God's will and His plan for our lives, no matter how challenging it might be. As Jon Courson puts it, "Prayer is not giving orders. It's reporting for duty."

Another practical step is to be mindful of how we treat others. Instead of engaging in fighting, quarreling, or gossiping, let's aim to be peacemakers. That means being slow to anger, quick to listen, and careful with our words. It's about choosing to build others up rather than tearing them down. By fostering a spirit of humility and kindness, we not only reflect God's love but also create a more peaceful environment around us. These small changes can lead to big transformations both within our hearts and in our relationships.

Now, let's talk about John the Baptist. He's a remarkable example of humility and pure motives. Even with a large following, John always directed the spotlight away from himself and toward Jesus, the "Lamb of God, who takes away the sin of the world" (John 1:29, NIV). The Bible describes him as a man whose "clothes were made of camel's hair, and he had a leather belt around his waist. His food was locusts and wild honey" (Matthew 3:4, NIV). Can you imagine? While we're often searching for the softest, most comfortable fabrics, John willingly wore camel's hair—a material far from comfortable. This choice wasn't random; it was intentional. It spoke volumes about his commitment to a life of simplicity, repentance, and detachment from worldly comforts. John wasn't worried about elevating himself or seeking personal comfort; his focus was on his divine mission to prepare the way for Jesus.

When some of John's disciples noticed that people were flocking to Jesus, they were concerned. But John, with incredible humility, reminded them, "A person can receive only what is given them from heaven. You yourselves can testify that I said, 'I am not the Messiah but am sent ahead of him'" (John 3:27-28, NIV). And then, in a statement that should challenge us all, he said, "He must become greater; I must become less" (John 3:30, NIV). John's entire life was about elevating Jesus while minimizing himself.

Final Thought:

Just as John found joy and purpose in his role within God's plan, we too can find satisfaction when we focus on serving God with pure motives. So, whether in our prayers, our service, or our daily interactions, let's strive to honor God and uplift others. Let's make sure our actions reflect a heart that seeks His glory above all else, trusting that He will use us in ways we can't even imagine.

Look at the description of John in Matthew 3:4 and his response in John 3:27-30. What can we learn from John's attitude towards his role and mission?

What does John 3:30 mean to you in the context of your own life? Are there areas in your life where you need to become less so that Christ can become greater?

KEY CONCEPTS FOR SPIRITUAL GROWTH
JAMES 4:1-3

DESIRE:

In the context of this passage, "desire" refers to a strong longing or craving for something one does not have. These desires, often driven by selfish motives or fleshly cravings, lead to internal conflicts and external strife. They contrast with godly desires, resulting in quarrels and dissatisfaction rather than peace and contentment.

COVET:

To "covet" means to have an intense and wrongful desire for something that belongs to someone else. In this passage, coveting is associated with jealousy and greed, leading to conflicts and disputes when people cannot obtain what they deeply long for. Coveting goes beyond mere desire; it involves an envious longing that disrupts relationships and leads to destructive behavior.

57

NOTES:

. . . .

. . . .

. . . .

. . . .

. . . .

. . . .

READ: JAMES 4:4-10 | HOSEA 1 & 3
HE IS JEALOUS FOR YOU

Before we dive into this next portion of Scripture, let's pause and consider a few things. When James refers to "adulterous people," he's not merely talking about physical adultery but rather a spiritual unfaithfulness. He's drawing a parallel to how Jesus views His relationship with the church, His bride. Just like in the Old Testament, the term "adulterous" was used to describe the Israelites when they turned away from God to chase after idols and other gods. This metaphor paints a vivid picture of how spiritual unfaithfulness can be likened to marital infidelity, breaking the covenant we have with God.

Now, let's take a closer look at the word "world" in verse four. The Greek word "kosmos" here is multifaceted. In some contexts, like John 3:16, "kosmos" refers to humanity—God's creation that He loves so much He sent His only Son to save. It's an all-encompassing term that reflects God's expansive love for all people. But "kosmos" also has another side, often pointing to the material and temporal things of life—money, power, possessions—that can distract and lead us away from God.

In James 4:4, we find yet another use of the word. Here, "kosmos" refers to a system of values, beliefs, and practices that are fundamentally at odds with God's ways. It represents the worldly attitudes and pursuits that prioritize self-interest, materialism, and desires over spiritual devotion. James warns us that "friendship with the world is enmity against God." This means aligning ourselves with worldly values puts us at odds with God. It's not about rejecting the people of the world, but rather the sinful systems and practices that draw us away from our faith.

Paul echoes a similar thought in 1 Corinthians 5:10, reminding us not to separate ourselves from people who sin but to guard against the influences that can corrupt our faith. Jesus Himself often sat with those society labeled as sinners and outcasts, engaging with them in love and compassion. He didn't isolate Himself but rather exemplified how to live in the world without being of it. So, James isn't contradicting other scriptures. He's not saying we should isolate ourselves but that we must guard our hearts against adopting values that contradict our faith.

The story of Hosea beautifully illustrates this concept. God commanded Hosea to marry Gomer, a woman who would be unfaithful to him, as a living metaphor of Israel's unfaithfulness to God. Despite Gomer's betrayal, Hosea's relentless love for her mirrors God's unwavering love and grace for His people. Even when we stray and prioritize worldly pursuits, God's love calls us back, offering grace and a chance for repentance. It's a powerful reminder that no matter how far we drift, God's love remains constant, inviting us to return.

James 4:6-7 speaks to this grace: "But he gives us more grace. That is why Scripture says: 'God opposes the proud but shows favor to the humble.' Submit yourselves, then, to God. Resist the devil, and he will flee from you." This grace isn't just a free pass; it's a powerful invitation to humble ourselves, turn away from sin, and draw closer to God. It's about recognizing our need for His mercy and acknowledging that, without Him, we can do nothing.

Imagine a husband waiting at home while his wife spends more and more time with her friends. He loves her, trusts her, but over time, he starts to feel neglected. His desire for her attention isn't about control; it's about a deep, loving commitment to their relationship. This scenario mirrors the relationship God desires with us. The Holy Spirit within us yearns for our devotion and affection, much like a faithful spouse desires the love of their partner. God's jealousy isn't a petty emotion; it's a profound longing for a relationship where we are fully committed to Him, just as He is to us.

But here's the incredible part: God doesn't just leave us in our wanderings. He gives us more grace. And sometimes, this grace comes through hardships and challenges. These trying times serve as reminders of our dependence on His love and grace. Just like Hosea's love for Gomer, God uses these experiences to strip away the distractions and idols in our lives, drawing us back to Him. It's not always easy or comfortable, but it's necessary for our growth and spiritual maturity.

This refining process, though often uncomfortable, is an expression of God's unwavering love and commitment. It's His way of ensuring we stay in relationship with Him, free from worldly entanglements and fully devoted to His purpose. So, when James tells us to "change your laughter to mourning," it's a call to repentance—a shift from a careless, self-indulgent attitude to one of humility and submission to God. It's a reminder that true joy and fulfillment are found in a life fully committed to Him, not in the fleeting pleasures of this world.

By embracing this call to repentance, we align ourselves with God's will, allowing His grace to transform us from the inside out. It's a journey of shedding the old, worldly ways and embracing a life of holiness, dedicated to reflecting His love and truth in everything we do. So, let's take this opportunity to examine our hearts, turn away from the things that pull us away from God, and fully commit ourselves to the relationship He desires with us. This is where true peace and joy are found—in the loving arms of our faithful God, who never stops pursuing us with His grace.

Final Thought

The story of Hosea and Gomer beautifully illustrates God's unwavering commitment to us. Like James, it calls us to turn back to Him, despite our failings. True joy and fulfillment aren't found in the fleeting pleasures of this world but in a life anchored in God's truth and grace. Let's stay vigilant, rooted in His love, and fully devoted to our walk with Him.

How does the term "adulterous people" relate to spiritual unfaithfulness, and why is it compared to marital infidelity?

? What does it mean to be a "friend" of the world in this context?
How can we live in the world without becoming part of it?

. . . .

. . . .

. . . .

. . . .

. . . .

. . . .

. . . .

. . . .

. . . .

. . . .

KEY CONCEPTS FOR SPIRITUAL GROWTH
JAMES 4:4-10

ADULTEROUS PEOPLE:

In this context, "adulterous people" is a metaphorical term referring to those who are unfaithful to God by pursuing relationships or alliances with worldly values and systems. Just as adultery in marriage is a betrayal of one's spouse, spiritual adultery is a betrayal of one's commitment to God. It indicates a divided loyalty, where individuals are drawn away from their devotion to God in favor of the world.

FRIENDSHIP:

"Friendship" here refers to a close association or alignment with the values, practices, and priorities of the world. In this passage, friendship with the world means adopting a mindset that prioritizes worldly desires and standards over God's ways. Such friendship indicates a compromised allegiance to God, leading to spiritual enmity with Him.

ENEMY:

An "enemy" in this context is someone who opposes or stands in direct conflict with God. When a person chooses to align themselves with the world and its values, they place themselves in opposition to God's will and purposes. Becoming an enemy of God implies a rejection of His authority and a resistance to His ways, leading to spiritual estrangement from Him.

NOTES:

READ: JAMES 4:11-12 | LUKE 18:9-14
DON'T SLANDER ONE ANOTHER

There's a certain kind of magic that envelops our family when we gather around the table for game night. Trivial Pursuit is our game of choice, and it's been that way since the children were little. We've always played in teams, ensuring that everyone has a fair chance to win. Amidst the clinking of plates and the laughter that leaves us breathless, we've unknowingly discovered a powerful lesson in love. You see, when we're united as a team, patience and kindness flow naturally. There's no room for jealousy or envy when a teammate scores a point, and we're never angry when they miss one. Sure, we might tease our opponents in a lighthearted manner, but for those on our team, we offer encouragement, cheer, and share in their triumphs. Hand in hand, we strive for the prize.

James echoes this sentiment in verse 11, urging believers to speak well of each other. He reminds us that when we slander our brothers and sisters in Christ, we're not just hurting fellow believers; we're also challenging God's law. In doing this, we put ourselves above the law, which clearly instructs us to love our neighbors as ourselves

For the entire law is fulfilled in keeping this one command:
"Love your neighbor as yourself. (Galatians 5:14, NIV)

Instead of honoring the law, we act as if we're the judges, a position only God can hold. This is a powerful reminder that our true calling is to live humbly, love others, and leave judgment to God.

With that said, when are we to judge others, if ever? The judgment called for in passages like Matthew 18:15-17 and Galatians 6:1 is meant to be constructive. It's about holding one another accountable within the church community—not to condemn, but to restore and guide. This type of judgment is exercised with humility, recognizing that all believers are under God's authority and are called to encourage each other toward righteousness. We're also called to be discerning and rightly divide the truth of God's word.

The judgement that James refers to in this chapter is destructive. This kind of judgment often stems from pride and self-righteousness, where individuals assume the role of judge—a role that belongs to God alone. It's about condemning others or speaking ill of them, thereby challenging God's law of love. The Apostle Paul also touches on this in 1 Corinthians 4:1-5, emphasizing that it is the Lord who judges and that we should not judge prematurely, as only God can reveal what is hidden and expose the true motives of the heart.

Jesus illustrated this contrast in the Parable of the Pharisee and the Tax Collector (Luke 18:9-14). The Pharisee, confident in his own righteousness, judged the tax collector, boasting of his own deeds. Meanwhile, the tax collector, aware of his own sinfulness, humbly asked for God's mercy. Jesus declared that the tax collector, not the Pharisee, went home justified before God. This parable vividly demonstrates that God values a humble and repentant heart over self-righteousness and judgment.

When I'm reading the Bible, I catch myself pointing the finger at times. I think, "Yeah, she does this, and yes, he does that," forgetting that I'm the one that needs to be changed by God's word. One thing that's helped me break this habit is remembering something an old man at our church used to say: "When you point a finger at someone, there are three fingers pointing back at yourself." This simple yet profound reminder encourages me to examine my own heart and actions before judging others. It helps me to focus on the grace I've received and to extend that same grace to others.

Final Thought

As Christians, we are called to love our neighbors as ourselves (Mark 12:31) and to approach others with a spirit of humility and grace. Let us remember that our role is not to condemn one another but to love and uplift one another, leaving judgment in the hands of God, who alone is righteous and just.

? What is the difference between constructive judgment (as seen in Matthew 18:15-17 and Galatians 6:1) and destructive judgment (as warned against in James)?

. . . .
. . . .
. . . .
. . . .
. . . .
. . . .
. . . .
. . . .
. . . .
. . . .

? As you study this section, what is one key takeaway that you can apply to your spiritual growth this week?

. . . .
. . . .
. . . .
. . . .
. . . .
. . . .
. . . .
. . . .

KEY CONCEPTS FOR SPIRITUAL GROWTH
JAMES 4:11-12

SLANDER:

In this passage, slander refers to making false or malicious statements about a brother or sister in Christ, which not only harms them, but also disrupts the unity and love that should characterize the Christian community.

JUDGE:

To judge in this context means to criticize or condemn someone, assuming a position of moral superiority. When one judges another, they place themselves in a position reserved for God alone, who is the ultimate Lawgiver and Judge. The passage warns against taking on this role, as it reflects a failure to recognize God's authority and undermines the principle of mercy and humility.

LAW:

The "law" in this passage refers to God's commandments, particularly the command to love one another, as Jesus taught. When someone judges another, they are, in effect, judging the law itself—suggesting that they are above the law. This is a form of arrogance, as the passage emphasizes that only God, the true Lawgiver, has the authority to judge. The law calls for love, mercy, and humility, and judging others contradicts these principles.

NOTES:

READ: JAMES 4:13-17 | 2 SAMUEL 7
SEEKING GOD'S DESIRE FOR US

I got a dollhouse for my birthday last Spring. Now, I've wanted one ever since I was a little girl, and finally, this year, it happened—a two-story Victorian character home, the kind you dream about. The only thing was, I had to put it together. "I should have this ready to go in a week, maybe two," I said, feeling confident in my ability to get things done quick.

But four months later, I'm still knee-deep in paint, stain, and glue, trying to bring this little house to life. Just the other day, I told my sisters that it's probably going to take me a year to finish. I'm not nearly as confident as I was four months ago because I've learned something along the way: Even the simplest projects can take more time and patience than we expect. And isn't that just like life? We think we've got it all figured out, but then the unexpected happens, and suddenly, we're reminded that our plans aren't always as straightforward as we'd hoped. It's in those moments that we realize how much we need to approach our plans with humility, trusting that God's timing and guidance are what truly matter.

James writes, "Now listen, you who say, 'Today or tomorrow we will go to this or that city, spend a year there, carry on business and make money.' Why, you do not even know what will happen tomorrow. What is your life? You are a mist that appears for a little while and then vanishes." (James 4:13-14, NIV)

James brings us back to the importance of prayer and the attitude we must have when seeking God's guidance. He's addressing that subtle but dangerous presumption that we know what's best for ourselves. The truth is, we don't even know what will happen five minutes from now—let alone tomorrow or next year. So how can we possibly determine the best path to take without God? This realization should humble us, reminding us of our deep and daily dependence on Him.

Earlier in James chapter 4, we talked about examining our motives before we come to God in prayer. Are we genuinely seeking His will, or are we just chasing after the things that we want? Are we more focused on our desires, or are we asking God what He desires for us? These are the questions that help us align our hearts with His purpose.

Whenever we're making decisions that shape our future, we need to consider God's will first and bring our concerns to Him in prayer. By doing this, we acknowledge His sovereignty and trust that He knows what's best for us, even when we can't see the full picture. It's this humble approach that ensures we're not leaning on our own understanding, but rather, we're submitting to God's wisdom and guidance, allowing Him to direct our paths.

Look at 2 Samuel chapter 7. David had plans—good ones. He wanted to honor God with a permanent dwelling place. But God had different plans. Through the prophet Nathan, God told David that he wouldn't be the one to build the temple; instead, his son Solomon would fulfill that role.

David's response to God's decision is just as noteworthy as his original desire to build the temple. Instead of reacting with disappointment or frustration, David praised God for His goodness and sovereignty. He expressed deep gratitude for all that God had done for him and his family, acknowledging that God's plans were far greater than his own.

David's willingness to set aside his own aspirations in favor of God's will teaches us invaluable lessons about humility and obedience. It reminds us that God's plans are not just different—they are always better, always good.

Final Thought

This chapter reminds us that even our most sincere and well-meaning plans must be submitted to God's will. It encourages us to let go of pride and presumptions and trust that God's wisdom surpasses our own.

? When God redirects your plans, as He did with David, how do you respond? What steps can you take to trust and follow God's guidance, even when it leads you down an unexpected path?

? How does acknowledging the uncertainty of life (as mentioned in James 4:14) help you rely more on God's wisdom rather than your own understanding?

KEY CONCEPTS FOR SPIRITUAL GROWTH
JAMES 4:13-17

BOAST:

In the context of this passage, to boast means to speak with excessive pride or self-satisfaction about one's own achievements, plans, or abilities. It reflects an attitude of self-reliance and arrogance, particularly in making plans without acknowledging God's sovereignty. James criticizes this kind of boasting because it disregards the uncertainty of life and the need to submit to God's will. Boasting in this manner is seen as sinful because it elevates human pride over humility and trust in God.

For example, someone might say, "Next year, I'm going to start a business, expand it across multiple cities, and make a lot of money. Nothing can stop me!"

This statement reflects boasting because it confidently assumes control over the future without considering the uncertainty of life or acknowledging that success ultimately depends on God's will. The person speaks with pride, relying solely on their own plans and abilities, rather than submitting their plans to God's guidance and recognizing His sovereignty.

NOTES:

Chapter 5

• LIVING FAITHFULLY THROUGH PERSEVERANCE •

READ: JAMES 5:1-6 - | LUKE 12:13-21
TREASURES THAT LAST

When we had our first baby, I was thrilled about getting things ready, especially the adorable clothes he would wear. Those tiny undershirts, snug sleepers, and oh-so-cute outfits—not to mention the precious little socks. With five older sisters, grandmas, and friends, Brendan was blessed with an abundance of clothes. Even after 32 years, I still remember his Winnie the Pooh sleeper, complete with a hoodie and little bear ears.

I never realized how quickly a newborn could grow until I found myself carefully packing his clothes into boxes as he outgrew them week by week. Before I knew it, we had a growing mountain of boxes downstairs, filled with enough sleepers and bibs to clothe a whole group of quintuplets—possibly two!

One day, my sister Kathy got the exciting news that she was going to be a grandma. I finally had someone to give the clothes to and a way to free up space in our basement. I was more than happy to haul the boxes upstairs where I could show off the collection I had lovingly saved. As I opened the boxes, however, my heart suddenly sank. The cardboard smelled musty, and the beautiful clothes I had stored were covered in mold. It was disappointing to say the least.

While that experience taught me to store linen in plastic bins, it also served to remind me that the things of this world are short-lived. They rot, they rust, they're eaten by moths... and because they're failing, they will always fail us.

As I got to thinking about that today, I was reminded of the Parable of the Rich Fool. In Luke 12:13-21, Jesus tells the story of a wealthy man who, after a bountiful harvest, decides to tear down his barns and build bigger ones to store all his grain and goods. He plans to relax and enjoy life, thinking he has secured his future. But God calls him a fool, saying, "This very night your life will be demanded from you. Then who will get what you have prepared for yourself?" The rich man failed to recognize that his wealth could not secure his soul or his eternal future.

This isn't to say that saving for the future, and planning for retirement, is wrong. The Bible encourages us to be wise stewards of the resources God gives us. What James is addressing in this section is the danger of placing our trust in wealth, believing it can provide ultimate security or fulfillment. Not because wealth itself is bad, but because one's reliance on it is a dangerous path. Instead, our focus should be on cultivating a heart that values integrity, generosity, and a deep relationship with God.

Benson Commentary offers a vivid depiction of the political climate during the time of James's writing. He describes how the unbelieving Jews, driven by a love of sensual pleasure and greed, often oppressed the poor. To warn these individuals and urge them toward repentance, James vividly portrays the imminent suffering that the Roman Empire, as an instrument of divine judgment, was set to inflict upon the Jewish people. Benson states,

> *The unbelieving Jews, being exceedingly addicted to sensual pleasure, and very covetous, were of course grievous oppressors of the poor. Wherefore, to alarm these wicked men, and, if possible, to bring them to repentance, James, in the first paragraph of this chapter, sets before them, in the most lively colours, the miseries which the Romans, the instruments of the divine vengeance, were about to bring on the Jewish people, both in Judea and everywhere else, now deserted of God for their crimes, and particularly for the great crime of murdering the Just One, Jesus of Nazareth, their long-expected Messiah. He highlights the futility and moral failure of accumulating wealth through injustice, knowing that it would soon be lost due to the impending Roman conquest.*

It's just as easy today to fall into this trap, especially in a culture that measures success by material wealth and possessions. The allure of luxury, comfort, clicks, and status can lead us to place too much value on things that have no lasting significance. Everything is but a breath, a fleeting whisper in the wind; even the strongest structures and the finest treasures have their time, and then they're gone, just like everything else around us.

This transient nature of life calls us to look beyond what is temporary, urging us to seek what is eternal and unchanging. It invites us to cultivate a heart that values integrity, generosity, and a deep relationship with God. When we prioritize these eternal treasures, we discover a richer, more meaningful life—one that isn't swayed by the ups and downs of our financial circumstances. This perspective keeps our focus on what truly matters, even amidst the shifting sands of a transient world.

Final Thought

In this chapter, we see a powerful warning directed at those who place their trust in material wealth. James vividly describes the temporary nature of riches, using images of rotting wealth, corroded gold and silver, and moth-eaten clothes to remind us that earthly possessions are fleeting and cannot provide true security.

James 5:4-6 condemns those who have gained wealth through unjust means, particularly by oppressing the poor. In today's society, what are some ways people might accumulate wealth at the expense of others?

What are some ways that the culture around us encourages the pursuit of wealth and material goods? How can you resist the temptation to measure your success by worldly standards?

KEY CONCEPTS FOR SPIRITUAL GROWTH
JAMES 5:1-6

TESTIFY:

In the context of James 5:3, "testify" means to provide evidence or serve as a witness against someone. The passage describes how the corroded gold and silver will "testify" against the rich, symbolizing how their decayed wealth will stand as evidence of their greed, corruption, and failure to use their resources justly. The wealth they hoarded, now worthless and corrupted, will serve as a witness to their moral and spiritual decay, ultimately condemning them.

SLAUGHTER:

"Slaughter" is often associated with judgment or punishment. The imagery of "fattening yourselves in the day of slaughter" suggests that the rich, in their pursuit of luxury and self-indulgence, are unknowingly preparing themselves for a day of reckoning or judgment, much like animals being fattened before they are slaughtered. It implies that their unchecked greed and indulgence will lead to their ultimate downfall and destruction.

NOTES:

READ: JAMES 5:7-12 | JOB 1-2 & 42
PATIENT IN TRIALS

Last summer was a rough one for me. We were finally over the pandemic, but so much had changed in its wake. Our business closed its doors, our boys lost their jobs, and they moved out together, taking the dog with them. Michael got sick, and we had to sell our house. With only two weeks to find a new place, we ended up an hour away from the kids. Through it all, I did my best to be thankful and positive. I thanked God for the new paths He was laying before us, particularly for the trials that seemed to gnaw at my peace.

One day, it all hit me. Sitting in my broken-down car on the side of a highway in the middle of nowhere, I poured out my pain to the Lord. I'm not ashamed to admit that I cried that day, because I've come to understand that sharing our struggles with God is a vital part of deepening our relationship with Him. When we walk in faith, trials will come—heavy burdens that threaten to crush our spirit, clouds that block out the sun, and tests that seem relentless. But here's the truth we need to hold on to: adversity will either leave us feeling defeated, or it will strengthen us.

David understood this. In Psalm 13, we witness him pouring his heart out to God in the midst of his own distress. Yet, at the end of his prayer, we also see his unwavering trust in the Lord:

> *But I trust in your unfailing love; my heart rejoices in your salvation. I will sing the Lord's praise, for he has been good to me. (Psalm 13:5-6, NIV)*

That same trust in God's unfailing love is echoed in James 5:7-12. Here, James encourages us to be patient in our suffering, pointing us to the examples of the prophets and the endurance of Job. He begins with a call to patience, likening it to a farmer waiting for his plants to grow. The harvest, he reminds us, cannot be hurried; it comes in its own time:

Be patient, then, brothers and sisters, until the Lord's coming. See how the farmer waits for the land to yield its valuable crop, patiently waiting for the autumn and spring rains. (James 5:7, NIV)

Just as the farmer waits for the rains, we too must wait on the Lord, trusting in His perfect timing. The trials we face are not without purpose; they are opportunities for us to cultivate patience and to strengthen our hearts as we look forward to the Lord's return.

James also urges us not to grumble against one another during these trials but to stand firm. The patience we practice in the face of hardship is a testament to our faith. He reminds us of the prophets who spoke in the name of the Lord, enduring suffering with patience:

As you know, we count as blessed those who have persevered. You have heard of Job's perseverance and have seen what the Lord finally brought about. The Lord is full of compassion and mercy. (James 5:11, NIV)

Job's story is a powerful example of the perseverance James is talking about. Despite losing everything—his wealth, his health, and even his children—Job remained faithful to God. He questioned, he grieved, but he never abandoned his trust in God. And in the end, God restored Job, blessing him even more than before.

As we face our own struggles, whether it's being stranded on the side of a road or something far more challenging, let's keep James's words close to our hearts. Our trials are not the end of the story. They are part of God's process of cultivating a faith within us that is strong, enduring, and steadfast.

Final Thought

Hold on to these powerful words: "The Lord is full of compassion and mercy." Whatever you're going through today, know that God sees your struggle, and He is working in and through it for your good and His glory.

? James suggests that trials have a purpose in cultivating patience and strengthening our hearts. How do you think trials accomplish this in our lives?

. . . .

. . . .

. . . .

. . . .

. . . .

. . . .

. . . .

. . . .

James 5:7-12 encourages a long-term perspective, focusing on the Lord's coming. How does maintaining an eternal perspective help us endure temporary hardships?

KEY CONCEPTS FOR SPIRITUAL GROWTH
JAMES 5:7-12

PATIENT:

In this context, "patient" refers to the ability to endure difficult circumstances or delays without losing faith or becoming agitated. It is the quality of waiting with calmness and trust, especially for the Lord's coming or during times of suffering.

PERSEVERE:

"Persevere" means to continue steadfastly in a course of action despite facing difficulties or opposition. It highlights the endurance and persistence of those, like Job and the prophets, who remained faithful to God even in the face of significant challenges and suffering.

SWEAR:

In this context, "swear" refers to making a solemn or serious promise or oath, often invoking God or something sacred as a witness to the truth of one's words. The passage advises against swearing by heaven, earth, or anything else's, instead one's word should be simple and truthful—"Yes" or "No"—without the need for elaborate oaths. This emphasis reflects the importance of honesty and integrity in speech.

NOTES:

JAMES 5:13-20 | 1 Kings 17:1-7 & 18:41-46
THE POWER OF FERVENT PRAYER

I remember those days when my kids were younger. I'd ask them to check if the water was boiling on the stove, and more often than not, they'd respond with something like, "I'm not sure. I see some bubbles coming up." And my answer to them was always the same: "When it's boiling, you'll know it's boiling. There's no mistaking it."

And you know what? That's how our prayer life should be—so intense and passionate that there's no mistaking we've been in the presence of God.

James 5:16-18 says, "The prayer of a righteous person is powerful and effective. Elijah was a human being, even as we are. He prayed earnestly that it would not rain, and it did not rain on the land for three and a half years. Again, he prayed, and the heavens gave rain, and the earth produced its crops."

Elijah's story is incredible, not because he was some superhuman, but because he was just like us—flesh and blood, with fears and doubts. But his prayers? They were unmistakable because they were fueled by his deep connection with God and his unshakable faith.

Think about it. Elijah's first prayer, asking for a drought, was no small thing. For three and a half years, not a drop of rain fell. That drought wasn't just inconvenient; it brought the whole nation to its knees. But here's the thing: Elijah didn't pray that prayer lightly. He prayed it because he knew it was in line with God's will. His prayer was about more than just stopping the rain—it was about turning the hearts of the people back to God.

And when the time was right, Elijah prayed again—this time for rain. But he didn't just throw up one quick prayer and walk away—he prayed persistently, seven times, sending his servant each time to check the sky. And when that tiny cloud finally appeared, Elijah knew God was about to move.

That kind of persistence is something we need to grasp hold of. Sometimes, we pray and expect an immediate answer, but God calls us to keep praying, to keep believing. It's not about twisting God's arm—it's about building our faith, aligning our hearts with His, and trusting in His perfect timing.

Elijah prayed with faith. He didn't wait for the rain to start before he believed; he prayed with expectation, knowing that God would fulfill His promise. And that's how we should pray too—with faith, believing that God hears us and will answer.

James 5:13-15 challenges us to pray in every circumstance—whether we're in trouble, joyful, or in need of healing. Prayer isn't just our last resort; it's our first response. In both drought and rain, Elijah prayed earnestly. And in every season of our lives, whether it's a season of hardship or blessing, we're called to do the same.

But there's another crucial piece to this. James 5:16 reminds us that the prayer of a righteous person is powerful and effective. Now, none of us are perfect, but walking in right relationship with God—turning away from sin and seeking His will—makes our prayers even more effective. Psalm 66:18 tells us plainly, "If I had cherished sin in my heart, the Lord would not have listened."

Elijah's life shows us the power of a fervent, faith-filled, and righteous prayer. His prayers brought both drought and rain, showing us just how mighty prayer can be when it's aligned with God's purposes.

So, let's take Elijah's example to heart. Let's commit to a prayer life that's unmistakably fervent—like boiling water. Let our prayers be full of passion, faith, and righteousness. Let's not hold back or be half-hearted. Let's pour ourselves out before God, trusting that He hears us and will act according to His perfect will.

Whatever you're facing—whether it's a small need or a major breakthrough—pray with the same fervency that Elijah had. Trust that God is listening, and that your prayers, just like Elijah's, have the power to move mountains. Remember, it's not about how eloquent your words are; it's about the earnestness of your heart and the righteousness of your walk with God.

Final Thought

In every situation, whether you're facing a drought or eagerly awaiting the rain, let your prayers be fervent, persistent, and filled with faith. Just as Elijah's prayers changed the weather, our prayers have the power to change our lives and the lives of those around us.

Elijah prayed seven times before the rain came. What does this teach you about the importance of persistence in prayer? Can you share an example where persistence in prayer made a difference in your life?

Psalm 66:18 reminds us that sin can hinder our prayers. How do you ensure that your heart is aligned with God, and how does this alignment affect your confidence in prayer?

KEY CONCEPTS FOR SPIRITUAL GROWTH
JAMES 5:13-20

FAITH:

Faith refers to a strong belief and trust in God and His promises, even when circumstances are uncertain. In this context, a prayer offered in faith has the power to bring healing and restoration, as it demonstrates reliance on God's ability to act according to His will.

CONFESS:

To confess means to openly acknowledge or admit one's sins or wrongdoings. In this passage, believers are encouraged to confess their sins to one another, creating an atmosphere of accountability and support, leading to spiritual healing and forgiveness.

RIGHTEOUS:

Righteous refers to being morally right or justifiable, living in accordance with God's standards. In the passage, a "righteous person" is someone whose life aligns with God's will, and their prayers are described as powerful and effective because of their close relationship with God and their commitment to living a godly life.

NOTES:

ANSWER KEY

Please note that the answers provided are intended to guide your understanding, but they may vary depending on personal perspectives. Many of these questions invite thoughtful reflection, and your responses might differ from the ones given here. My goal is to encourage you to consider the teachings and how they apply to your own life and faith journey.

CHAPTER 1

What are some situations in which you felt God was "pruning" you in the past? And, how have these experiences helped you grow in your faith and bear fruit?

This answer will be different for everyone.

James encourages believers to consider trials as 'pure joy' because they produce perseverance. How can this understanding shape your perspective on current or future challenges?

It can shift our perspective from viewing challenges as burdens to seeing them as opportunities for spiritual growth. This mindset helps us approach difficulties with a sense of purpose, knowing that enduring these trials strengthens our faith and builds character, ultimately drawing us closer to God.

Can you identify areas where you might be struggling to fully trust God's wisdom and guidance, and how can you apply James 1:5-8 to grow in faith during these moments?

This answer will be different for everyone.

What practical steps can you take to ensure that your decisions are rooted in faith and aligned with God's will, especially when facing trials or challenges?

Practical steps include regular prayer for guidance, seeking wisdom from Scripture, consulting with mature Christians, and being sensitive to the Holy Spirit's prompting. It's also essential to wait patiently for God's direction and remain open to His will, even when it differs from our desires.

Why do you think Jesus told the rich man to sell all of his possessions? What was he teaching him by saying that?

Jesus told the rich man to sell all his possessions to challenge his attachment to wealth and to expose the condition of his heart. Jesus was teaching that true discipleship requires placing God above all earthly possessions and that wealth can be a hindrance to fully committing to God's kingdom.

In Mark 10:21, Jesus told the rich young ruler, "One thing you lack." What do you think that "one thing" was?

The "one thing" the rich young ruler lacked was complete surrender to God. Although he followed the commandments, his attachment to wealth revealed that he had not fully given his heart to God. Jesus was highlighting the need for wholehearted devotion and willingness to sacrifice everything for the sake of following Him.

Reflect on a time when a seemingly small thought or desire led to a sin in your life. Looking back on it now, what could you have done to stop it?

This answer will be different for everyone.

What is "renewing your mind" and how can it help you resist temptation?

"Renewing your mind" involves aligning our thoughts and attitudes with God's truth through regular engagement with Scripture, prayer, and meditation on His Word. This process helps us resist temptation by transforming our thinking, enabling us to discern right from wrong and making us more receptive to the guidance of the Holy Spirit.

How can being "quick to listen, slow to speak, and slow to become angry" transform your relationships with others? Can you think of a recent situation where practicing these principles could have led to a more positive outcome?

a) This practice fosters better communication and understanding in relationships. It shows respect for others' perspectives, reduces misunderstandings, and helps create a more peaceful and loving environment, reflecting the character of Christ.

b) This answer will be different for everyone.

How does effective listening reflect the love and wisdom that God desires in us?

We demonstrate love by valuing others' thoughts and feelings, showing that we care about them. It reflects wisdom by allowing us to respond thoughtfully and compassionately, aligning our actions with God's desire for us to be understanding, empathetic, and slow to judge.

What are some areas in your life where you've noticed something that needs to be addressed but haven't yet taken action?

This answer will be different for everyone.

What specific steps can you take to avoid being like the priest and the Levite, who knew the truth but failed to act on it?

We can commit to taking action when we see someone in need. Specific steps include cultivating a heart of compassion, being willing to inconvenience ourselves for the sake of others, and prioritizing love over ritual or personal comfort. Regularly praying for a compassionate heart and seeking opportunities to serve others can help us live out the truth of God's love in practical ways.

CHAPTER 2

What are some modern-day examples of favoritism in our communities or churches? How can we guard against this in our own lives?

Some examples might include: a wealthy donor receiving special recognition during a church service while smaller donors are overlooked, a church consistently calling on the same volunteers for important tasks while not giving others the opportunity to serve, or a church youth group planning activities that only cater to one specific clique. And of course, cliques of any kind where there is a failure to consider the inclusion of others.

To guard against this, we can regularly examine our attitudes and actions, strive to treat everyone with equal respect and kindness. Being intentional about including and valuing those who might otherwise be overlooked is key to avoiding favoritism.

In what ways have you noticed yourself showing favoritism, either in your family, friendships, or church community? How can you work towards being more inclusive?

This answer will be different for everyone.

What is the difference between belief and faith? How does understanding this difference influence the way we live out our faith in practical ways?

Belief is an acceptance that something is true, while faith goes a step further by acting on that belief, trusting in God's promises even when we cannot see the outcome. Understanding this difference helps us to live out our faith more actively, encouraging us not only to believe in God but also to trust Him in our daily lives, make decisions based on His guidance, and take steps of obedience, even when it's challenging.

Can you share a time when someone's actions spoke louder than their words in your life?

This answer will be different for everyone.

CHAPTER 3

Colossians 4:5-6 encourages us to have conversations "full of grace, seasoned with salt." What does this look like in practice, especially when interacting with those who don't share our faith?

It's speaking with kindness, respect, and love, even when discussing difficult topics. It involves being considerate of the other person's perspective, avoiding harsh or judgmental language, and sharing truth in a way that is compassionate and thoughtful.

This approach can open doors for meaningful dialogue and allow the light of Christ to shine through our interactions.

Can you recall a situation where holding your tongue led to a better outcome? How did this decision affect your situation?

This answer will be different for everyone.

How does Jesus' example of washing the disciples' feet, including those who would betray or deny Him, challenge our approach to serving others?

This answer will be different for everyone.

Think about a recent act of service or kindness you performed. What was your motive behind it, and how can you continue to grow in aligning your actions with the humility and selflessness exemplified by Jesus?

The first part of this answer will be different for everyone.

We can grow in aligning our actions with Jesus' humility and selflessness by regularly studying His life and teachings, praying for a heart that reflects His character, and seeking opportunities to serve others without seeking recognition. Practicing gratitude, putting others' needs before our own, and being willing to sacrifice for the sake of others are practical ways to embody Christ's humility in our daily lives.

CHAPTER 4

Look at the description of John in Matthew 3:4 and his response in John 3:27-30. What can we learn from John's attitude towards his role and mission?

John's attitude demonstrates humility and clarity of purpose. He understood that his role was to point others to Christ, not to seek his own comfort and glory. John's willingness to decrease so that Christ could increase teaches us the importance of recognizing our place in God's plan and being content with the mission God has given us, without seeking recognition or comparison.

What does John 3:30 mean to you in the context of your own life? Are there areas in your life where you need to become less so that Christ can become greater?

This answer will be different for everyone.

How does the term "adulterous people" relate to spiritual unfaithfulness, and why is it compared to marital infidelity?

The term "adulterous people" relates to spiritual unfaithfulness by depicting a betrayal of our commitment to God. Just as marital infidelity involves breaking a sacred trust between spouses, spiritual adultery involves breaking our covenant relationship with God by turning to the world or other idols. This comparison emphasizes the seriousness of placing anything above our devotion to God.

What does it mean to be a "friend" of the world in this context? How can we live in the world without becoming part of it?

Being a "friend" of the world means aligning ourselves with worldly values, desires, and practices that are opposed to God's will.

To live in the world without becoming part of it, we must remain rooted in God's Word, seek His guidance in our decisions, and prioritize our relationship with Him above all else. This involves making conscious choices to avoid compromising our faith and values, even when pressured by the culture around us.

What is the difference between constructive judgment (as seen in Matthew 18:15-17 and Galatians 6:1) and destructive judgment (as warned against in James)?

Constructive judgment involves lovingly correcting someone with the goal of restoring them to a right relationship with God and others. It's done with humility and a desire for the person's well-being, as seen in Matthew 18:15-17 and Galatians 6:1. Destructive judgment, as warned against in James, is critical and condemning, often rooted in self-righteousness or pride, and it tears others down rather than building them up.

As you study this section, what is one key takeaway that you can apply to your spiritual growth this week?

This answer will be different for everyone.

When God redirects your plans, as He did with David, how do you respond? What steps can you take to trust and follow God's guidance, even when it leads you down an unexpected path?

This answer will be different for everyone.

How does acknowledging the uncertainty of life (as mentioned in James 4:14) help you rely more on God's wisdom rather than your own understanding?

Acknowledging the uncertainty of life reminds us of our limited control and the need to depend on God, who knows all things. This awareness encourages us to seek His guidance in all our plans and decisions, trusting in His wisdom rather than leaning on our own limited understanding or assumptions about the future.

CHAPTER 5

James 5:4-6 condemns those who have gained wealth through unjust means, particularly by oppressing the poor. In today's society, what are some ways people might accumulate wealth at the expense of others?

In today's society, people might accumulate wealth at the expense of others by underpaying workers, exploiting labor in developing countries, engaging in corrupt business practices, or manipulating markets to their advantage. These practices often prioritize profit over the well-being of individuals and communities.

What are some ways that the culture around us encourages the pursuit of wealth and material goods? How can you resist the temptation to measure your success by worldly standards?

The culture around us often glorifies wealth and material success through advertising, social media, and entertainment, which can create pressure to accumulate possessions and status symbols. To resist this temptation, focus on spiritual values, prioritize relationships and experiences over material goods, and regularly remind yourself of the biblical truth that true success is measured by faithfulness to God rather than worldly achievements.

James suggests that trials have a purpose in cultivating patience and strengthening our hearts. How do you think trials accomplish this in our lives?

Trials help cultivate patience and strengthen our hearts by teaching us to rely on God, developing perseverance, and refining our character. As we navigate challenges, we learn to trust God's timing and grow in our ability to endure difficult circumstances, which deepens our faith and resilience.

James 5:7-12 encourages a long-term perspective, focusing on the Lord's coming. How does maintaining an eternal perspective help us endure temporary hardships?

Maintaining an eternal perspective helps us endure temporary hardships by reminding us that our current struggles are not the end of the story. It shifts our focus from immediate difficulties to the hope of Christ's return and the promise of eternal life, providing comfort and motivation to remain steadfast in our faith, knowing that our suffering is temporary and that God's ultimate plan for us is good.

Elijah prayed seven times before the rain came. What does this teach you about the importance of persistence in prayer? Can you share an example where persistence in prayer made a difference in your life?

Elijah's persistence in prayer teaches us the importance of continuing to seek God's intervention, even when we don't see immediate results. It encourages us to remain steadfast and patient, trusting that God hears our prayers and will answer in His perfect timing. Persistence in prayer reflects our faith and dependence on God.

Psalm 66:18 reminds us that sin can hinder our prayers. How do you ensure that your heart is aligned with God, and how does this alignment affect your confidence in prayer?

To ensure that our heart is aligned with God, we need to regularly confess our sins, seek forgiveness, and strive to live in obedience to His Word. This alignment with God helps to clear any barriers in our relationship with Him, allowing us to approach Him with confidence, knowing that our prayers are heard and that we are seeking His will rather than our own.

Made in United States
Orlando, FL
23 September 2024

51833141R00059